尾田栄一郎

Hello and thank you for taking our bus tour. We're heading toward the 100th chapter of *One Piece*. On your right, you can see the thumbs held up high. There's plenty more action and adventure ahead!

-Eiichiro Oda, 1999

E iichiro Oda began his manga career at the age of 17, when his one-shot cowboy manga **Wanted!** won second place in the coveted Tezuka manga awards. Oda went on to work as an assistant to some of the biggest manga artists in the industry, including Nobuhiro Watsuki, before winning the Hop Step Award for new artists. His pirate adventure **One Piece**, which debuted in **Weekly Shonen Jump** in 1997, quickly became one of the most popular manga in Japan.

ONE PIECE VOL. 11
EAST BLUE PART 11

SHONEN JUMP Manga Edition

This graphic novel contains material that was originally
published in English in **SHONEN JUMP** #39–41.

STORY AND ART BY EIICHIRO ODA

English Adaptation/Lance Caselman
Translation/JN Productions & Michie Yamakawa
Touch-up Art & Lettering/Mark McMurray, Vanessa Satone
Additional Touch-up/Josh Simpson
Design/Sean Lee
Editor/Yuki Takagaki

Printed in the U.S.A.

Published by VIZ Media, LLC
P.O. Box 77010
San Francisco, CA 94107

20
First printing, July 2006
Twentieth printing, November 2023

ONE PIECE

Vol. 11
THE MEANEST MAN IN THE EAST

STORY AND ART BY
EIICHIRO ODA

Arlong

Nami
A thief who once specialized in robbing pirates. Although she hates pirates, Luffy convinced her to be his navigator.

Monkey D. Luffy
Boundlessly optimistic and able to stretch like rubber, he is determined to become King of the Pirates.

Usopp
His penchant for tall tales is matched by his accuracy with a slingshot. His father, Yasopp, is a member of "Red-Haired" Shanks's crew.

THE STORY OF ONE PIECE
Volume 11

Monkey D. Luffy started out as just a kid with a dream—and that dream was to become the greatest pirate in history! Stirred by the tales of pirate "Red-Haired" Shanks, Luffy vowed to become a pirate himself. That was before the enchanted Devil Fruit gave Luffy the power to stretch like rubber, at the cost of being unable to swim—a serious handicap for an aspiring sea dog. Undeterred, Luffy set out to sea and recruited some crewmates: master swordsman Zolo, treasure-hunting thief Nami, lying sharpshooter Usopp, and Sanji, the high-kicking chef.

Johnny

Yosaku

Genzo

"Red-Haired" Shanks

Nojiko

Searching for Nami, Luffy and his crew head to Arlong Park, stronghold of the ferocious Fish-Man Pirates, only to discover that Nami herself is one of them! They learn the story of Belle Mère and the origin of Nami's hatred of pirates from Nami's stepsister, Nojiko, who also explains how Nami swallowed her hatred and went to work for Arlong, gathering loot to buy her village's freedom.

Moved by Nami's secret suffering, Luffy goes toe to toe with Arlong, but is hurled into the ocean! Sanji and the others fight and defeat Arlong's men and rescue Luffy. But they still have to contend with the most terrible foe of all—Arlong himself!

Sanji
The kind-hearted cook (and ladies' man) whose dream is to find the legendary sea, the "All Blue."

Roronoa Zolo
A former bounty hunter and master of the "three-sword" fighting style. He plans to become the world's greatest swordsman.

Vol. 11
THE MEANEST MAN IN THE EAST

CONTENTS

Chapter 91: DARTS

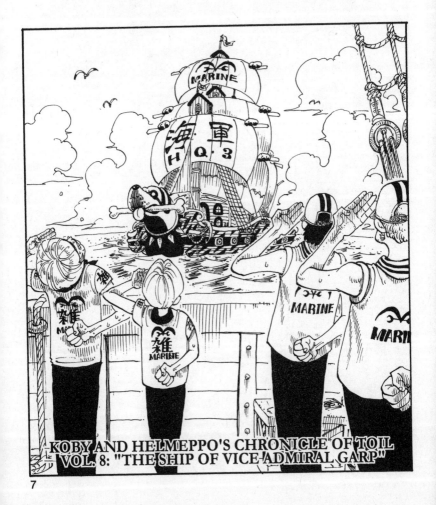

KOBY AND HELMEPPO'S CHRONICLE OF TOIL
VOL. 8: "THE SHIP OF VICE ADMIRAL GARP"

8

SH WAK!!!

HOW DARE YOU MOCK ME!!!

UGH!!!

AAAGH!! I'VE BEEN BEATEN BY A FISH!!!

CHONK

I'M NOT FOOLING AROUND!!

!!

CHONK

THAT'S WHAT YOU GET FOR FOOLING AROUND!!!

12

WHUMP .... **!!**

...**!!**

SHLUP...

I DOUBT HE KNEW THAT. IT HAD TO BE DUMB LUCK.

IF HE'D TAKEN ONE STEP BACK, HE WOULD'VE LOST THAT ARM!

ARE YOU OKAY, LUFFY !!?

WOOOO

WOOOO

WOOOOOO

...

SH LUK

DO OM!!!

HUH?

HUFF...
HUFF...

WHERE'D HE GO!?

THE WATER...

LUFFY, HE'S IN THE WATER!!!

WHAT?

HE WENT UNDER.

GURGLE...

IT'S ARLONG!!!

WHUP!

HEY, A SHARK!!!

NOBODY CAN BEAT ME IN THE WATER! I'M EVEN FASTER IN MY OWN ELEMENT!!!

GLUP

GLUP

WOOOoo

WOO·OOo

HMM...

YOU WITHSTOOD MY ATTACK.

OOOOOH...

plip plip...

...YOUR TORMENT CONTINUES!!!

SHE·EN

BUT THAT JUST MEANS...

SHC!!

OM!!

SHARK DARTS!!!!

24

NO WAY !!!

WHAT ARE YOU DOING!? HE'S GONNA ATTACK AGAIN!! RUN!!

NO.

plup

plup...

BROTHER LUFFY, YOU HAVE TO RETREAT!!

...

WOOOOO-O

I'M GONNA KNOCK HIM OUT !!!

I'M GONNA GET HIM.

DOOM!! DOOM!!

GLUP

GLUP

⑥ INSTEAD OF THE SBS QUESTION CORNER, HERE'S A CUT-AWAY VIEW OF LUFFY'S SHIP, THE MERRY GO. A LOT OF READERS HAVE ASKED ABOUT IT.

THE MERRY GO

7. (p164)
Luffy's Cabin

5. (p124)
Gun Deck
and Anchor
Rope Storage

2. (p66)
Men's Quarters

8. (p164)
Nami's Tangerine Grove

1. (p46)
Conference Room, Galley, and Bridge

3. (p84)
Storeroom and Battery Deck

6. (p144)
Bathroom

4. (p104)
Women's Quarters

Chapter 92: HAPPINESS

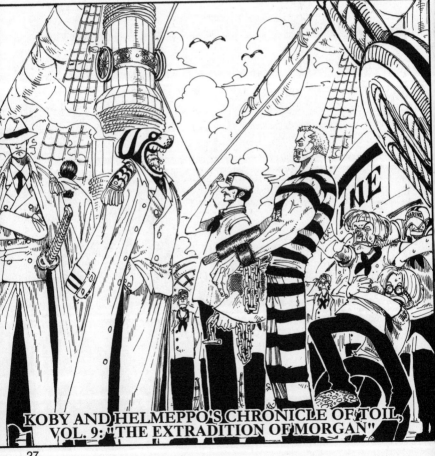

KOBY AND HELMEPPO'S CHRONICLE OF TOIL,
VOL. 9: "THE EXTRADITION OF MORGAN"

WOOOOOO

OR HAVE YOU GIVEN UP?

GLUP

YOU'VE GOT GUTS, HUMAN.

GLUP

COME ON...

...YOU LOUSY SHARK !!!

WO oo

TUMP!

GUM GUM ...

... SHIELD !!!

YOU'RE TAKING THE FULL FORCE OF HIS ATTACKS!!

DON'T YOU UNDERSTAND WHAT "HIDE" MEANS, LUFFY!!?

IF HE HITS YOU AGAIN, YOU'RE DOOMED !!!

WO ING

DOES HE THINK THAT'LL PROTECT HIM?

WHAT'S THAT?

SHARK...

SHWOO

I'LL SKEWER HIS WORTHLESS HEART !!!

I'M GOING TWICE AS FAST THIS TIME !!!

OOOG

FISH-MEN ARE EXCELLENT AT GATHERING OCEANIC DATA, BUT WITHOUT A GOOD CARTOGRAPHER IT'S WORTHLESS.

THIS ISN'T JUST PAPER.

NO ONE ELSE IN THE WORLD CAN DRAW SUCH ACCURATE MAPS.

THESE ARE CHARTS. NAMI SPENT THE LAST EIGHT YEARS DRAWING THEM.

I SEE.

NAMI'S A GENIUS.

...HAS BLOOD ON IT.

THIS PEN...

THERE'S NOTHING MORE TRAGIC AND STUPID THAN WASTING ONE'S GIFTS!!

ONCE WE HAVE CHARTS OF ALL THE WORLD'S OCEANS, NOTHING CAN STOP THE FISH-MEN!!

DRAWING CHARTS FOR ME ALLOWS NAMI TO DO THE THING SHE LOVES BEST!!!

THE WHOLE WORLD WILL BE MY KINGDOM!!!

AND SOON I WILL ACHIEVE MY AMBITION!!!

THINK YOU CAN USE THAT GIRL AS WELL AS I DO!!?

I SEE...

...THE EAST BLUE!!!

THIS ISLAND IS THE STEPPING STONE TO...

KLAK...

...WON'T MOVE !!!

WHAT!? MY SAW ...

!?

WOOo...!!

TUP...

DOOM!!

KREK KREK

"USE"?

1. Lounge

Conference Room, Galley, and Bridge

ⓒ Room for meetings and discussions

ⓒ The crew gathers here for meals and breaks.

Galley (Brick-walled)

Whipstaff (for steering)

Lamp

Refrigerator

Provisions

Rack for wine and Beer

This ship isn't steered with a wheel. The whipstaff that's attached to the tiller turns the rudder and steers the ship right or left.

Whipstaff

Rudder

Chapter 93:
GOING DOWN

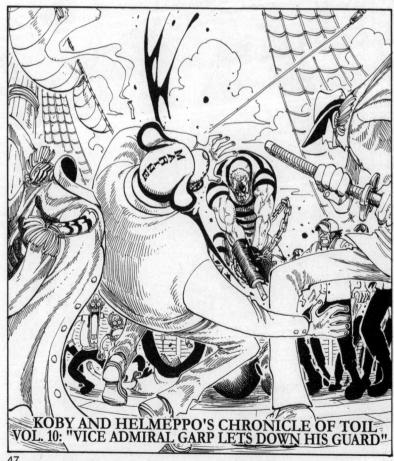

KOBY AND HELMEPPO'S CHRONICLE OF TOIL
VOL. 10: "VICE ADMIRAL GARP LETS DOWN HIS GUARD"

K LANG!!!

MY SHARK SAW... !!!

...NAMI IS, ANYWAY?

WHAT DO YOU THINK...

THWAK..!!

BAM..!!

BLAST YOU!! WHAT ARE YOU DOING !!!?

LUFFY ...?

KRASH..!!

KRESH..!!

KA

BA THOOM..!!

BAM..!!

BLAST!! MY CHARTS!!

FWUP

FWUP

!! THUD THUD..

THUD

TH— WA M!! UMF!!!

MY SEA CHARTS!!!

AND DON'T LEAVE THIS ROOM UNTIL YOU'RE DONE!! GOT THAT !!?

HERE'S THE NEW INFORMATION. NOW GET CRACKING ON THOSE CHARTS!!

THUD' THUD..

YOU DREW THIS CHART WRONG ON PURPOSE !!!

YOU NASTY GIRL! YOU CAN'T FOOL ME!!

THUD

KRASH!!

KLONK!

UNH !!!

CURSE YOU! YOU'RE DESTROYING EIGHT YEARS OF NAMI'S WORK!!!

AGH!!

huff huff

WHAP!

BWAH HA HA HA HA!!

NOJIKO...!!!

BELLE-MÈRE...!!

KA-BOOM

THAT'S SOME FIGHT!

...

WHA

GAAGH!!!

!?

... THANK YOU.

...

IT'S OVER.

KLAK KLAK KLAK

PARKING PA

WHAT IS IT!!? WHAT'S GOING ON!!?

CHO

...!!!

THROB THROB

YOU'VE SEALED YOUR FATE, RUBBER BOY!!!

...CAN BRING DOWN ARLONG PARK!!!

GET AWAY FROM THOSE CHARTS!!! NO PUNY HUMAN...

GWAHH!

SHARK...

...
TOOTH
DRILL
!!!!

BAM!!!

WOO

...
BATTLE
AXE
!!!!

REEEEE

KRASH!!!!

!!!!

WOO WOOOOO

HUFF...
HUFF...

HUFF
HUFF

HUFF

HUFF
!

SNAP!

HUFF

HUFF

BUT LUFFY'S STILL IN THERE!!!

NAMI!! C'MON!!

WATCH OUT, EVERY-BODY!! GET BACK!!!

IT'S GONNA COLLAPSE!!!

THIS IS CRAZY!!

LOOK!! THE SHOCK WAS TOO MUCH!! ARLONG PARK'S ...!!!

WUZZZ

RRNMMBB

KREEK!!

RRNMMBB
WUZZZ

KLAK

KLAK
KLUNK

HUH?

2.

Men's Quarters

Grog & water casks

Wardrobe

Sofa (for relaxing in comfort)

Coffee table (for relaxing in comfort)

Mast

Laundry Baskets

Open to descend

Mast

ⓐ Bedroom and lounge for Luffy, Zolo, Usopp, and Sanji

ⓑ Messy, But that's okay Because it's for men.

Hammocks (five for guests)

Emergency exit (connects to the women's quarters)

Washing equipment (each man does his own laundry)

Chapter 94:
THE OTHER VILLAIN

WHAT HAPPENED IN THERE!!?

WHOA ...!!

ARLONG PARK IS IN RUINS!!!

LUFFY ...

WITH EVERYTHING DE-STROYED, YOU DON'T THINK...?

WHO WON!!?

*TRANSLATION: BROTHER LUFFY!!!

IS HE ALL RIGHT?

pLUP...

pLUP...

NAMI!!!

...?

UH-HUH!!!

PLIP!!

...

MR. GENZO!!

WHUP

IT'S LIKE A DREAM. I NEVER THOUGHT I'D SEE THIS DAY.

TA-DAH

HE DID IT, NOJIKO!! HE WON!! ♡

HE WON!!

HOORAY

ARLONG PARK HAS FALLEN!!!!

HEE HEE HEE !!

DA-DOOM!!!

HYIK HYIK HYIK HYIK !!!

!!?

HOLD EVERY-THING !!!

IT COULD'VE BEEN A FLUKE, BUT SOMEHOW YOU TWO-BIT PIRATES...

...DEFEATED THE FISH-MEN.

MARINE

IT'S MY LUCKY DAY!!!

I SAW THE WHOLE THING. WELL DONE.

HIM!!

THROW DOWN YOUR WEAPONS!!! YOUR VALIANT DEEDS...

...WILL GO ON THE RECORD OF CAPTAIN NEZUMI OF NAVY UNIT 16!!!

NOW, THANKS TO YOU, THE GOLD I WAS SUPPOSED TO GIVE TO ARLONG...

...AND ALL THE TREASURE IN ARLONG PARK, ARE MINE!!!

DOOM!!!

!!!?

KRUNCH

KRUNCH

KRUNCH

AAAAGH!!!

DON'T BE A WET BLANKET.

WE'RE CELEBRATING OUR VICTORY.

ZOLO!!

HE STILL DOESN'T GET IT.

YOU'D BETTER NOT MESS WITH ME. I'LL MAKE YOU REGRET IT.

...AND WRECKING BELLE-MÈRE'S TANGERINE GROVE.

THIS IS FOR SHOOTING NOJIKO...

HUH!?

PLOP!

!!!!?

SPLASH

CAPTAIN
!!!

HIT HIM A
THOUSAND
TIMES
MORE!!

THANK
YOU,
NAMI!

I FEEL
BETTER
NOW.

HEY, WHAT'LL WE DO IF SOMETHING TERRIBLE REALLY DOES HAPPEN!!?

THAT'S NOT IT, YOU IDIOT.

HOW DID HE KNOW ABOUT ME BECOMING KING OF THE PIRATES?

YOU MARK MY WORDS

HE SAYS SOMETHING TERRIBLE'S GOING TO HAPPEN.

YOU NEVER KNOW...

HMPH. WHO'D HAVE IMAGINED WE'D BE SAVED BY PIRATES?

LET'S TELL EVERYONE ON THE ISLAND THE GOOD NEWS!!!

COME ON, EVERYONE!!! WE SHOULDN'T BE CELEBRATING ALL BY OURSELVES!!!

YAHOO!!!

ARLONG PARK HAS BEEN DESTROYED!!!

IT TOOK EIGHT YEARS, BUT FINALLY...

...EVERYBODY'S FREE!!

SPLOOSH

IT'S ALL OVER, BELLE-MÈRE.

OF COURSE NOT!!

I'M SURE SHE WOULDN'T HAVE WANTED HER PRECIOUS DAUGHTER JOINING THOSE SEA-WOLVES.

WOULD YOU HAVE LISTENED IF SHE'D TRIED TO STOP YOU?

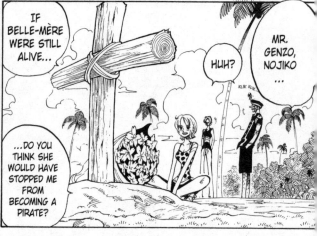

IF BELLE-MÈRE WERE STILL ALIVE...

...DO YOU THINK SHE WOULD HAVE STOPPED ME FROM BECOMING A PIRATE?

HUH?

KLIK KLIK

MR. GENZO, NOJIKO...

ABSO-LUTELY NOT!!!

BLEH !!!

80

IT'S CRAZY THAT HE CAN EVEN MOVE.

YEAH, BUT IT'D TAKE A NORMAL PERSON TWO YEARS TO RECOVER...

THE IDIOT.

BLAB BLAB

AAARRGH!!

THEY'RE STILL AT IT.

YACK YACK

WHY A MUSICIAN?

...BUT A MUSICIAN SHOULD COME FIRST, RIGHT?

A DOCTOR? THAT WOULD BE NICE...

IS THERE A DOCTOR ON YOUR SHIP?

YOU NUMBSKULL! TRYING TO FIX SUCH A SERIOUS INJURY YOURSELF!!

WELL, PIRATES SING, DON'T THEY?

OUCH...

ZZZ ZZZ

HA HA HA HAHA

...YOU'RE BELLE-MÈRE'S DAUGHTER, ALL RIGHT!!!

THERE'S NO DOUBT ABOUT IT...

WHY ARE YOU LAUGHING, MR. GENZO?

HA HA HA HA HA!!

HA HA HA...I CAN'T HELP IT!

3.

Storeroom &
Battery Deck

To the whipstaff in the conference room

Tiller

Tiller → To the rudder

Stairs to women's
quarters (latched hatch)

To the
Bathroom

Towels

Food storage

Cannon
There's another
one here (two
side ports).

ⓒ Grog casks, water
Barrels, food

ⓓ Treasure chests are also stored
here. Any treasure not taken By
Nami to her room is kept here.

Chapter 95:
SPIN, PINWHEEL

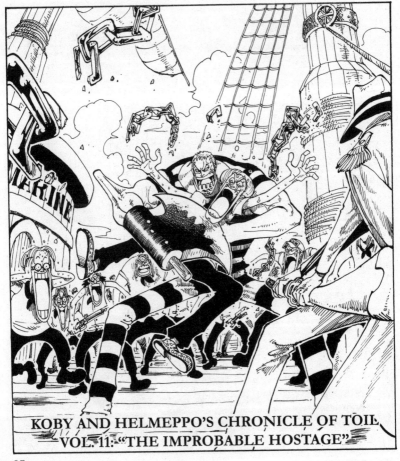

KOBY AND HELMEPPO'S CHRONICLE OF TOIL VOL. 11: "THE IMPROBABLE HOSTAGE"

NIGHT FELL AT LAST.

THE SEA WAS CALM ONCE MORE.

AH HAHAHAHA GAHAHAHA

SPLAP

THE WHOLE ISLAND CELEBRATED THAT NIGHT...

...AND CONTINUED ON THROUGH THE FOLLOWING NIGHT.

AH HA HA HA HA HA HA HA HA

EVERYONE WAS LIVING FOR THE MOMENT.

EVERYONE LIVED TO LAUGH.

SO IT'S TIME FOR US...

...TO LIVE OUR LIVES TO THE FULLEST AND LAUGH LIKE FOOLS!!!

THERE HAVE BEEN SO MANY SACRI-FICES.

HOLD IT, KID!!!

I'M GOING BACK.

TMP TMP TMP

AW, THERE'S NO FOOD HERE.

HUH?

...

BA-BUMP!

PROSCIUTTO AND HAM!!!

YEAH, SOMEBODY DIED...

GLUG

...A LONG TIME AGO.

MUNCH

MUNCH

?

IT'S A GRAVE... DID SOMEBODY DIE?

YEAH, THOSE.

IT'S "CONDO-LENCES."

... COMBO-NINSES... HUH?

MY COMBO-LENCES...

ACCEPT MY CONGO-LESES...?

...PLEASE ACCEPT MY CONGO-LENCES... *HUH?*

WELL, IN THAT CASE...

LISTEN, KID. NAMI'S GOING TO SAIL OFF WITH YOU PIRATES. IT WILL BE A DANGEROUS VOYAGE.

...

KLIK KLIK

KLIK...

I WOULDN'T DO ANY--

BUT IF YOU GUYS DO ANYTHING TO MAKE HER UNHAPPY, I'LL KILL YOU!!!!

I UNDERSTAND.

...

NOD

DO YOU UNDER-STAND !!!?

I THOUGHT THAT AT FIRST.

...BECAUSE THIS DIDN'T HAPPEN IN TIME TO SAVE YOUR FATHER.

I THOUGHT YOU'D BE UPSET...

YACK YACK

WHADDAYA MEAN?

HMPH. YOU'RE NO FUN.

WHAT DID I DO!!?

OW! OW! WHY ARE YOU PINCHING ME!!?

CHEEKY BOY.

KRER'K

ZING ZING

...REGRETS ARE A WASTE OF TIME.

THEN I REALIZED...

BEING A MEANIE'S FINE BY ME.

HA HA HA HA HA HA!!

YOU'RE DOING A GOOD JOB ALREADY!!

YOU TATTOOED MEANIE!!!

HMPH...

I WAS ALL SET TO PICK ON YOU AGAIN.

YACK

YACK

BA-BOOM BA-BOOM...

THAT'S HOW IT IS WITH TATTOOS.

NOT COMPLETELY.

YOU'LL ALWAYS HAVE A SCAR.

BOOM BOOM

WILL IT BE COMPLETELY GONE?

WA— HA HA HA HA HA HA

BONG BONG

...

IT'LL NEVER BE COMPLETELY GONE.

HMM ...

I'M NOT ONE OF THEM!! BUT NOW I'VE BEEN BRANDED A PIRATE!!!

I DON'T WANT ANYONE TO SEE MY TATTOO.

...

NAMI...

IT'S NOTHING. IT'S JUST A DECORATION.

SO WHAT?

NOJIKO!! YOU GOT A TATTOO!?

BUT...

HA HA HA HA HA!

I'M JUST LIKE YOU, NAMI.

HUH?

FWIP

HERE...

I WANT YOU TO GIVE ME THIS TATTOO.

DOCTOR...

SONG NO. 6, "USOPP'S CHEER"!

AH HA HA HA HA! THOSE TWO SURE CAN DANCE!

GA HA HA HA HA!!

YACK YACK

THE MORNING OF DEPARTURE...

BLAB BLAB

...WHO OWE HER!!

THAT FOOL. WE'RE THE ONES...

...ONCE HER MIND IS MADE UP, SHE WON'T BUDGE.

I TOLD HER TO TAKE AT LEAST A LITTLE MONEY, BUT...

TA-DOOM

HUH?

SET SAIL... NOW !!!!

NAMI!?

SHE SAID TO SET SAIL, SO LET'S DO IT.

SHE STARTED RUNNING. WHAT'S SHE UP TO!?

TO

MP

!!?

FWAP

RAISE THE SAIL!!!

NO WAY!!

...WITHOUT GIVING US A CHANCE TO THANK HER!?

DON'T TELL ME SHE'S GOING TO LEAVE...

LET US THANK YOU PROPERLY!!!

STOP, NAMI!!!

TMP TMP TMP TMP TMP

...

WAIT, NAMI!!! YOU CAN'T JUST LEAVE US LIKE THIS!!!

FWOOoM

GET MOV- ING !!

HEY, THEY'RE SAILING!!!

BUT WE WANTED TO THANK YOU GUYS ONE MORE TIME!!

SWIP SWIP SWIP

NAMI!!!

SHE SHOULD LEAVE THE WAY SHE WANTS.

ARE YOU SURE WE SHOULD LET HER DO THIS?

SHOOM ····!

NAMI!!!

TOMP!!

WHY!!?

SHE GOT US!!

HUH? WHAT'S THIS, DOCTOR?

LOOK AT THIS, MR. GENZO.

FWUP

HAVE FUN, NAMI.

HA HA

THAT SISTER OF MINE IS SOMETHING.

...AND A PINWHEEL, SHE SAID.

IT'S A TANGERINE...

SHE HAD THIS TATTOO DONE.

WHAT IS THIS SYMBOL?

HEH HEH... I WON'T BE NEEDING IT ANYMORE.

HUH? MR. GENZO, WHERE'S YOUR PINWHEEL?

4.

Women's Quarters

@ Nami's room It's clean

Emergency exit (connects with the men's quarters, but isn't normally used).

Treasure chest (precious jewels, Nami's collection)

Bookcase

Desk

Hammock storage (Pull the rope and a hammock descends.)

Stairs (enter from storeroom)

Storage Box for surveying and navigation tools

Grog

Bar

@ Merry (vol. 3, p. 148) designed this room for Usopp's friend Kaya, so it's nicely decorated.

@ It was built by a carpenter, Mr. Tell, before the ship left Coco Village.

Chapter 96:
THE MEANEST MAN IN THE EAST

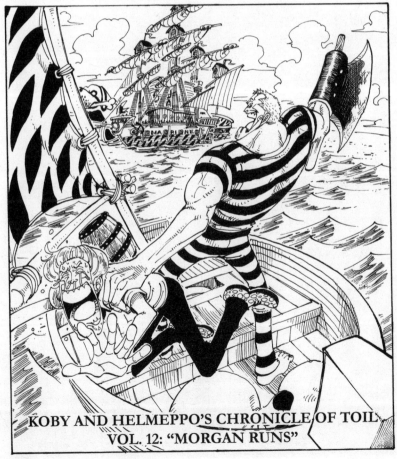

KOBY AND HELMEPPO'S CHRONICLE OF TOIL,
VOL. 12: "MORGAN RUNS"

YOU'RE CHARGING TOO MUCH!

DID YOU RAISE THE PRICE AGAIN?

WHAT'S A NEWSPAPER OR TWO?

IF YOU RAISE IT AGAIN, I'M NOT BUYING FROM YOU ANYMORE.

KAW

KLINK!

NEWS PAPER

STOP SQUAWKING!! I'M TRYING TO DEVELOP THE ULTIMATE KILLER, THE PEPPER SAUCE STAR!!

ANYONE WHO GETS THIS IN HIS EYES...

...IT'S TIME TO MAKE MONEY FOR MYSELF. I DON'T WANT TO BE A PENNILESS PIRATE.

DON'T BE STUPID! NOW THAT ARLONG'S GONE...

DO OM

YOU'RE DONE COLLECTING MONEY, AREN'T YOU?

IT ADDS UP IF YOU BUY ONE EVERY DAY.

KAW

NO!! WHAT? CAN'T I HAVE JUST ONE!? GAAA-AGH!!!

FWOOSH

AARGH!!! HANDS OFF!!! ...WON'T STAND A CHANCE!!

KRASH!!

SPLASH!

AW, THANK YOU, SANJI. ♡

NAMI, I SHALL GUARD THIS GROVE WITH ALL THE LOVE IN MY HEART!!

DOOM!!

THIS IS NAMI'S TANGERINE GROVE!! I WON'T LET YOU TOUCH THEM!!

OKAY. I'M IN TOO GOOD A MOOD TO FIGHT.

hee hee hee

FWUP!

THERE WAS ANOTHER COUP D'ÉTAT IN VIRA. THE WORLD SURE IS IN TURMOIL.

FWUP!

YAY! WE'RE FINALLY SAILING FOR THE GRAND LINE!! YEE-OWW!! SHE'S GOT HIM WRAPPED AROUND HER FINGER.

FWOOSH

AND AT LONG LAST, THE MERRY GO SAILS FOR THE GRAND LINE.

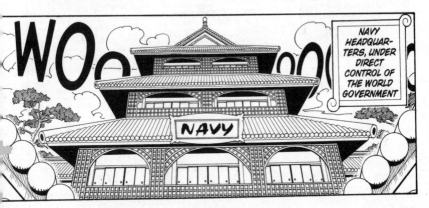

NAVY HEADQUARTERS, UNDER DIRECT CONTROL OF THE WORLD GOVERNMENT

...ARE UNABLE TO DEAL WITH THESE PIRATES?

SO YOU'RE SAYING THAT OUR BRANCH UNITS...

THAT IS CORRECT.

"SAW-TOOTH" ARLONG OF THE FISH-MAN PIRATES, 20 MILLION!!

DON KRIEG OF THE PIRATE ARMADA, 17 MILLION.

BUGGY THE CLOWN, 15 MILLION.

WANTED

DEAD OR ALIVE
ARLONG
20.000.000—
MARINE

WANTED

DEAD OR ALIVE
KRIEG
17.000.000—
MARINE

WANTED

DEAD OR ALIVE
BUGGY
15.000.000—
MARINE

...HAVE NOW BEEN SMASHED.

...BUT EACH OF THESE PIRATES IS WORTH OVER 10 MILLION. THEIR PIRATE RINGS...

THE AVERAGE REWARD IN THE EAST BLUE IS 3 MILLION BERRIES...

COMMANDER BRANDNEW
NAVY HEADQUARTERS

WHAAm!!
WANTED!!

STARTING A REWARD AT 30 MILLION IS UNPRECEDENTED...

WE MUST NIP THIS EVIL IN THE BUD BEFORE IT SPREADS!!!

...BUT WE BELIEVE IT'S NECESSARY.

DEAD OR A
MONKEY-D
30.000.000

THIS IS THE STRONGHOLD OF LIBERTY. IN THIS AGE OF PIRATES, NO WEAKNESS IS PERMITTED HERE!!!

ANYONE WHO WANTS TO LEAVE IS FREE TO DO SO!!!

WE ARE JUSTICE!!!

IT'S NOT THE FAULT OF THE CITIZENS IF THEY FALL PREY TO CUTTHROATS!!

...IT'S UP TO US, THE NAVY, TO USE OUR MIGHT TO CRUSH THEM!!!

IF EVIL FORCES SAIL THE SEAS...

THEY SAY WE'RE WORTH 30 MILLION BERRIES!!

HA HA HA HA!! WE'RE WANTED DEAD OR ALIVE!!

YOU'RE GRINNING LIKE AN IDIOT. IT'S NOTHING TO BRAG ABOUT.

LOOK!! I'M KNOWN ALL OVER THE WORLD!!

AT THAT PRICE, HEADQUARTERS IS PROBABLY INVOLVED. THE TOUGHEST BOUNTY HUNTERS ARE GOING TO COME AFTER YOU, TOO.

THE NAVY'S HUNTING YOU, LUFFY!!

AS USUAL, YOU GUYS HAVE NO IDEA HOW SERIOUS THIS IS.

DON'T BE JEALOUS! IF YOU GET TO BE A BIG SHOT, THEY MIGHT PUT YOU ON A POSTER TOO, EVEN IF YOU AREN'T A CAPTAIN.

HEY, THERE'S AN ISLAND.

YEAH!!

OKAY, LET'S SAIL FOR THE GRAND LINE, MEN!!

THIS IS NO TIME TO BE RELAXING IN THE EAST BLUE.

IF WE SEE THAT ISLAND...

THERE IT IS.

...THEN WE'RE APPROACHING THE GRAND LINE.

THE PIRATE KING, GOLD ROGER, WAS BORN THERE...

...AND EXECUTED THERE.

THAT'S WHERE THE FAMOUS ROGUETOWN IS.

THEY CALL IT "THE TOWN OF THE BEGINNING AND THE END."

WANT TO GO THERE?

IT'S WHERE THE PIRATE KING DIED!

ROGUE-
TOWN
TOWN OF
THE
BEGINNING
AND THE
END

DOOM

Roguetown

YACK
YACK

BLA
B
BLAB

SO THIS IS
WHERE THE
AGE OF
PIRATES
BEGAN.

WOW!!
THIS
PLACE IS
HUGE!!

I GUESS
I'LL FIND
US SOME
EQUIPMENT.

I CAN PROBABLY GET
SOME GOOD COOKING
INGREDIENTS HERE.

And
some cute
chicks.

TMP TMP

RIGHT!!
I'M GOING
TO GO
SEE THE
EXECUTION
SCAFFOLD
!!

I'LL BE
GLAD TO
LEND YOU
SOME
MONEY...
AT 300%
INTEREST.

HEH
HEH

THERE'S
SOMETHING
I WANT TO
BUY TOO.

OUR BOSS IS IN JAIL, THANKS TO YOU LOT. NOW YOU'RE GOING TO PAY.

SO...YOU'RE NOT WITH THAT MONSTER TODAY, EH!?

YACK YACK

BLAB BLAB

WELL, I'LL BE HAPPY TO TAKE YOU ON.

THEN YOU HAVEN'T HAD ENOUGH.

WOOO——...O

ALL RIGHT, THEN!!

WHAT!? YOU WANT TO FIGHT US!!?

...THAT BECAUSE OF HIM, OUR DREAMS OF ENTERING THE GRAND LINE ARE RUINED!!!

DIE! AND LET THAT MON-STER KNOW...

HUH?

WUP...

!! WO OOOo !!

SHW

SHUK

!!?

FWUMP!!

OUCH!

OH... OH... AH...

TUNK

KLAK

ARE THESE YOURS?

HEY.

OH.

FWEET FWEET

YOU SURE ARE STRONG, SISTER!!

YAY KLAP KLAP

OH! HUH?

BLUSH

YAY KLAP KLAP

AH HA HA HA!!

TH-THANK YOU VERY MUCH.

S-SORRY.

120

HUH?

HUMPH. I DON'T CHALLENGE ONE-ARMED HAS-BEENS.

GRRR...

I'M IN A BAD MOOD. YOU HERE TO CHALLENGE ME?

GRRR...

HAWK-EYE. THIS IS UNEXPECTED.

WHAT!!? NO WAY!!!

KLANK...!!

ABOUT A BOY IN SOME LITTLE VILLAGE...

HE REMINDED ME OF A STORY YOU TOLD ME LONG AGO.

I'VE FOUND AN INTERESTING PIRATE.

SO, YOU'RE HERE...

...LUFFY.

"RED-HAIRED" SHANKS
PIRATE CAPTAIN

FOOL!! HOW CAN I NOT DRINK ON A DAY LIKE THIS!?

GROG? BUT WHAT ABOUT YOUR HANGOVER!?

YOU DRINK UP TOO, HAWK-EYE!!

SEA DOGS!!! BREAK OUT THE GROG!!! WE'RE GONNA CELEBRATE !!!

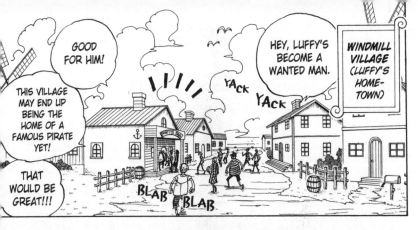

GOOD FOR HIM!

THIS VILLAGE MAY END UP BEING THE HOME OF A FAMOUS PIRATE YET!

THAT WOULD BE GREAT!!!

HEY, LUFFY'S BECOME A WANTED MAN.

WINDMILL VILLAGE (LUFFY'S HOME-TOWN)

YACK YACK

BLAB BLAB

ARE YOU WORRIED?

BUT IT WAS HIS DREAM.

A PIRATE'S A PIRATE!!

HEH HEH... LOOK HOW HAPPY LUFFY IS, MR. MAYOR.

Yeah!!

Party time!

KLUNK

SHUT UP, FOOL!! WHAT'S SO GREAT ABOUT HAVING THIS VILLAGE BE HOME TO A CRIMINAL!?

GRRR GRRR GRRr

IT'S THE MAYOR!!

...OR HIS DESTINY...

HIS DREAM...

5.

Gun Deck & Anchor Rope Storage

Life preservers
(they float like crazy)

Rope (essential on a sail ship)

Large oars
(This is a sailing
ship, But these
are needed
when there is no
wind. The crew
rows the ship
with these
huge oars!)

Cannon
(forward,
port !)

Anchor
rope

@ Capstan
(turn this to
raise the anchor)

Cannonballs

Gunpowder

Weapons
storage

Cleaning
equipment

@ This is basically a
storeroom for arms.

Capstan

There's a
compass on top.

This is how they
raise the anchor.

Chapter 97: KITETSU III

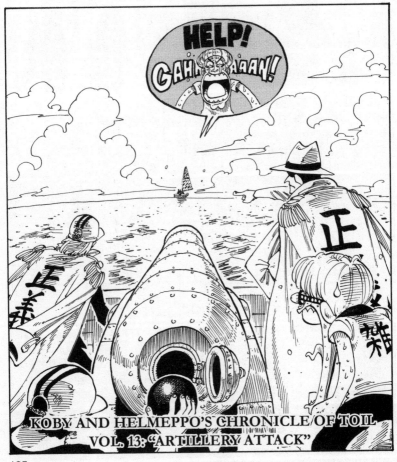

KOBY AND HELMEPPO'S CHRONICLE OF TOIL
VOL. 13: "ARTILLERY ATTACK"

DOOM!!!

THE EXECUTION SCAFFOLD...

BLAB BLAB

YACK YACK

BLAB BLAB

...WAS EXECUTED.

THAT'S WHERE GOLD ROGER...

YACK YACK

THAT'S IT.

...DIED RIGHT THERE.

BLAB BLAB

YACK YACK

THE GREATEST PIRATE OF ALL TIME...

THIS IS WHERE...

...THE GREAT AGE OF PIRATES BEGAN.

I WAS SO WEAK.

DARN IT!

YACK YACK

I DOUBT I'LL SEE HER AGAIN, THOUGH.

I GUESS FEMALE SWORDSMEN DO EXIST.

BLAB BLAB

STILL, I WAS WEAK.

STILL...

I-I'M SORRY.

AND SHE'S EVEN A SWORDS-MAN!

Like two peas in a pod.

IT'S UNCANNY HOW MUCH SHE LOOKS LIKE KUINA.

128

I WANT A SWORD.

AT A WEAPONS SHOP...

ARMS SHOP

OH YES! YES, YES, YES, YES!

OLD SWORDS, NEWER SWORDS, AND BRAND-NEW SWORDS. WE HAVE 'EM ALL...

...AND A SOLID REPUTATION OF OVER 200 YEARS IN THE BUSINESS!

TA-DAH

hee hee hee

swup swup

MATSU
WEAPONS SHOP OWNER

YES, YES. WELCOME!

PLEASE COME IN AND LOOK AROUND.

YOU'LL ONLY GET A BLUNT SWORD FOR 50,000...

...GOT IT!?

WHAT AN AMATEUR.

HM PH!

TWO SWORDS FOR 100,000 BERRIES!?

THIS GUY'S A BUM.

SWUMP

SELL ME TWO SWORDS.

I HAVE 100,000 BERRIES.

100,000?

THE SWORD AT HIS WAIST... COULD IT BE...!!?

...!!

I'LL TAKE WHATEVER YOU'VE GOT. I'M LOW ON CASH RIGHT NOW.

!

THIS IS IT!!!

DOOM!!

THIS IS... !!!

WHY ARE YOU SHAKING?

COULD I... HAVE A LOOK AT THAT SWORD?

ER...AH... COULD...

ACT NATURAL, ACT NATURAL...

?

WHAT?

THIS SWORD'S NO GOOD.

SWUP!!

WAIT! SORRY, I LIED.

THIS POOR SUCKER WALKED IN WITH A LEGENDARY SWORD! JUST TALK TO HIM CALMLY...!!

CALM DOWN!! THIS IS YOUR BIG CHANCE!!

HUH? WHAT ARE YOU TALKING ABOUT?

ER... FORGET THAT.

500,000 BERRIES THEN!!!

I'LL GIVE YOU 200,000 BERRIES FOR IT.

THEN YOU'LL HAVE 300,000 AND YOU CAN BUY THREE SWORDS FOR 100,000 BERRIES EACH!

LOOK HERE, FRIEND. MAYBE WE CAN WORK AROUND YOUR LACK OF FUNDS.

THIS SWORD IS NOTHING SPECIAL, BUT IT MIGHT BE WORTH *SOMETHING.*

LISTEN...

...THIS SWORD ISN'T FOR SALE AT ANY PRICE.

GAAAH

HOW CAN HE REFUSE!!?

I'LL GIVE YOU 650,000 BERRIES FOR IT!

WHAT THE HECK!?

I ALMOST HAVE HIM!

DON'T SAY IT!! DON'T SAY IT!!!

COULD IT BE...!!?

WHAT'S SHE DOING HERE!?

GULP!?

WHOA!!! THAT SWORD!!!

...THE WADO ICHIMONJI, THE STRAIGHT ROAD OF PEACE!!

THIS IS...

SURE, THAT'S ITS NAME...BUT IT'S NO GREAT SHAKES.

LOOK AT THIS BLADE!

"WADO" WHAT!?

⁉

JUST LOOK RIGHT HERE! THIS SWORD'S WORTH 10 MILLION BERRIES!!

TH ROB! THROB!! THROB!!!

"NO GREAT SHAKES"!? ARE YOU NUTS!? THIS IS ONE OF THE GREAT 21!! IT'S A FAMOUS SWORD!!

YOU'RE HERE TO PICK UP AUTUMN RAIN RIGHT!? I'VE POLISHED IT!!

DAMAGING YOUR BUSINESS!? I'M SORRY! DID I SAY SOMETHING WRONG!?

WHY, YOU... I'LL SUE YOU FOR DAMAGING MY BUSINESS!!!

YOU IDIOT! WHY'D YOU HAVE TO TELL HIM THAT!!?

EEK! WHOA! OH! WHUP

WHAM!!

WHAT'S A NOVICE LIKE YOU DOING WITH A FAMOUS SWORD, ANYWAY?

I'VE NEVER SEEN SUCH A BEAUTIFUL SWORD! I COULDN'T HELP MYSELF!!

BUT SHE'S RIGHT. THAT SWORD IS WASTED ON SOMEONE LIKE YOU WHO DOESN'T KNOW ITS VALUE.

THAT IDIOT GIRL SAVED YOU.

IT IS A FAMOUS SWORD!!

fwip!!

WHAT ARE YOU DOING !!?

LEAVE THAT SWORD AND GET OUT!!

KLAK KLAK KRASH!!

AAAH !!

I MET YOU ON THE STREET EARLIER!

HUH!?

PICK TWO.

THERE ARE SWORDS WORTH 50,000 BERRIES IN THAT BARREL.

WHAT'S HE SO MAD ABOUT?

BOUNTY HUNTER?

HAVEN'T YOU HEARD OF HIM? HIS NAME'S RORONOA ZOLO.

THREE SWORDS AT ONCE, HUH? JUST LIKE THAT BOUNTY HUNTER!

YOU MUST LIKE SWORDS!

THAT'S UNFOR-GIVABLE!!

USING A SWORD TO MAKE MONEY...

BUT IT'S AN EVIL NAME!!

THAT'S THE NAME OF A MASTER SWORDSMAN WHO'S FAMOUS THROUGHOUT THE EAST BLUE.

I KNOW THE NAME WELL.

AND MOST OF THE WORLD-FAMOUS SWORDS ARE IN THEIR HANDS.

ALL THE FAMOUS SWORDSMEN ARE EITHER PIRATES OR BOUNTY HUNTERS.

WHY IS THERE SO MUCH EVIL IN THE WORLD TODAY!?

THOSE SWORDS MUST BE CRYING.

THEN THAT MONSTER TOOK OVER THIS TOWN.

AND WHAT HAPPENED? THE CUSTOMERS STOPPED COMING.

I LIKE BAD GUYS!

THIS SHOP USED TO BE FILLED WITH MEN WHO WANTED TO SAIL THE GRAND LINE.

WELL, THERE ARE PROBABLY GOOD REASONS FOR THAT.

A MAN'S GOT TO DO WHAT HE CAN TO EAT IN THESE HARD TIMES.

DEVIL FRUIT!?

HE'S GOT THE POWER OF THE DEVIL FRUIT!!

CAPTAIN SMOKER IS NOT A MONSTER!!

THEN I'M GOING TO COLLECT ALL THE FAMOUS SWORDS THAT HAVE FALLEN INTO THE HANDS OF THE EVIL MEN OF THE WORLD.

I'LL GET THE 12 SUPREME GRADE SWORDS, THE 21 EXCELLENT GRADE SWORDS AND THE 40 FINE GRADE SWORDS...EVEN IF IT KILLS ME!!

IN ANY CASE, I'LL USE MY AUTUMN RAIN...

...TO HONE MY SKILLS AS A SWORDS-MAN!

136

THIS SWORD'S PREDECESSOR, KITETSU II, WAS AN EXCELLENT-GRADE SWORD!

IT'S WORTH A MILLION BERRIES!

WOW!! THIS IS A GENUINE FINE-GRADE SWORD!!

AND THE ORIGINAL KITETSU WAS A SUPREME-GRADE SWORD!!!

ER... YEAH.

...WERE 50,000 BERRIES EACH, RIGHT!?

HEY, MISTER, YOU SAID THESE SWORDS...

WOoOOoOO

THIS SWORD'S BE-WITCHED.

HUH? WHY NOT?

NO! NOT THAT ONE! I CAN'T SELL THAT ONE!!

THE FIRST KITETSU AND ITS SUCCESSORS ARE GOOD BLADES, BUT THEY'RE ALL CURSED!!

...!! WELL, YOU'RE RIGHT.

I CAN JUST TELL.

NO.

YOU'VE HEARD OF IT!?

THESE DAYS, NO SWORDSMAN IN THE WORLD USES A KITETSU...

...AND IF HE DID, HE WOULDN'T BE AROUND LONG.

FAMOUS SWORDSMEN HAVE DIED TRAGIC DEATHS BECAUSE THEY WIELDED THE KITETSU SWORDS.

HAH! THOUGHT YOU WERE...

...AN EXPERT, EH!?

SHOW OFF!!

AND I WAS SO PUSHY.

I DIDN'T KNOW IT WAS SO DANGER-OUS!!

...FOR-GIVE ME!!

...PLEASE...

...BUT I MIGHT BE CURSED FOR IT.

I'D LIKE TO GET RID OF THAT SWORD MYSELF...

ARE YOU A FOOL? I CAN'T SELL YOU THAT SWORD!! IF YOU DIED, IT'D BE LIKE I KILLED YOU MYSELF!!

I'LL TAKE IT!!

I LIKE THIS SWORD!!

...VERSUS THIS SWORD'S CURSE.

HOW 'BOUT THIS THEN?

MY LUCK...

WHY DON'T WE FIND OUT WHICH IS STRONGER?

YOU'RE THE FOOL! JUST GET RID OF THAT THING!!

WHAK!!

AAGH! HONEY BUN...

...AM I!!?

FWIP
FWIP
FWIP

IF I LOSE...

FWIP!

!?

...THEN I'M NOT MAN ENOUGH TO POSSESS IT...

OH!!!!

THAT BLADE'S RAZOR SHARP!!!

STOP FOOLING AROUND!! YOU'LL LOSE YOUR ARM!!!

I'LL TAKE IT.

HEY, WILL YOU CHOOSE ANOTHER ONE FOR ME?

SWIP

WOW...

HEY!!

JUST WAIT!!!

?

HEY, WAIT RIGHT THERE.

TMP-TMP-TMP

....!!!

O-OKAY.

HUH?

OUR SHOP IS NOTHING FANCY.

THIS IS THE BEST SWORD WE HAVE.

THIS SWORD HAS A BLACK LACQUERED SHEATH, AND THE BLADE HAS MIDAREBA.*

YUBASHIRI, OR SNOW CHASER, IS CATEGORIZED AS A FINE-GRADE SWORD. I'LL GUARANTEE ITS SHARPNESS!!

*A SWORD TERM FOR AN IRREGULAR PATTERN.

A SWORD CHOOSES ITS WIELDER.

I'LL PRAY FOR YOUR GOOD FORTUNE.

IT'S BEEN A WHILE SINCE I'VE LOOKED INTO THE EYES OF A REAL SWORDSMAN.

FORGIVE ME FOR TRYING TO TRICK YOU EARLIER.

AND YOU CAN HAVE THE KITETSU FOR FREE, OF COURSE.

NEVER MIND THE MONEY!! JUST TAKE IT!!!

HMM... BUT I CAN'T BUY IT. I TOLD YOU, I DON'T HAVE ANY MONEY.

...MAKES ME FEEL WHOLE AGAIN.

AHH, HAVING THREE SWORDS...

WOMEN DON'T UNDERSTAND ANYTHING!!

WELL, WELL. IMAGINE A MISER LIKE YOU GIVING AWAY YOUR SHOP'S TREASURES.

I- I CAN'T GET UP.

YES, DEAR!!!

GO CLEAN THE BATHROOM!!

WHAT'S WRONG WITH A MAN ENTRUSTING ANOTHER MAN WITH HIS DREAMS!!?

WE GOT A TIP ABOUT SOME PIRATES.

GO GET HER!!

AND HOW LONG'S THAT SUPPOSED TO TAKE!!?

SERGEANT TASHIGI WENT TO PICK UP A SWORD FROM THE SWORD SHOP.

ISN'T TASHIGI BACK YET!!?

ROGUE-TOWN NAVAL BASE, MAIN GATE

THAT WOMAN IS INSUFFERABLE!

SHE'S AN EMBARRASSMENT TO THE NAVY!

SHOOM DOOM!!

AYE-AYE, CAPTAIN SMOKER!!

I'VE GOT TO ADMIT, BIG CITIES HAVE A LOT GOING FOR THEM!!

FWOOO!

WHOO!!

YACK YACK

BLAB BLAB

WHAT A BEAUTY! ♡

WOW...

Chapter 98:
DARK CLOUDS

KOBY AND HELMEPPO'S CHRONICLE OF TOIL
VOL. 14: "A HINDRANCE TO THE ARTILLERY ATTACK"

ALL OF THEM!

I'LL TAKE... THESE!

?

COME AGAIN.

WIP WIP WIP

FUNK

HOW RUDE. OF COURSE I DO.

I HOPE YOU HAVE ENOUGH MONEY.

ALL OF THEM!?

FUNK

DO YOU HAVE A SHEET OF PLASTIC?

EXCUSE ME, MA'AM.

PLASTIC? BUT THE WEATHER'S FINE.

ANTIQUE

THERE'S A STORM COMING.

THE BAROMETRIC PRESSURE HAS DROPPED.

AW, I WANTED TO STROLL AROUND A BIT LONGER.

THE AIR'S DIFFERENT.

BLAB BLAB

YACK YACK

THAT'S THE SPECIAL EXECUTION SCAFFOLD! IT'S UNDER THE JURISDICTION OF THE WORLD GOVERNMENT!!!

DOOM!!

WHY?

KRU

NGH!!

COME DOWN RIGHT--

I'VE FOUND YOU AT LAST, LUFFY!! IT'S BEEN A LONG TIME!!

WAAAAAH!!

AAAH

WUMP...

GASP!

HEY, DON'T BE SO MEAN...

...MR. POLICE-MAN.

...WHAT WAS THAT?

HEY! LOOK OUT!

WHAT HAPPENED!!? THE FOUNTAIN WENT RIGHT PAST HER!!

...CAN NEVER BE MARRED. YOU NEEDN'T WORRY.

WOOOOOO

PARDON THE SPECTACLE, BUT HER SMOOTH, SILKY SKIN...

I AM THE EXQUISITE LADY ALVIDA!!

YOU LOOK KINDA DIFFERENT...

REALLY?

YOU SILLY FOOL!!

RIGHT HERE!! IT'S ME!!

ALVIDA!? WHERE IS SHE!?

I PARTOOK OF THE SLIP-SLIP FRUIT!!

NOW MY BEAUTIFUL SKIN CANNOT BE MARRED BY ANY ATTACK!!!

HEH HEH! NICE OF YOU TO NOTICE!

I ATE THE DEVIL FRUIT AND TRANSFORMED!!!

...WAS BARELY ENHANCED. HOWEVER, AS YOU SAID...

SADLY, MY BEAUTY...

WE TEAMED UP IN ORDER TO FIND YOU.

...THERE'S SOMEONE YOU MUST DEFEAT FIRST!!

BUT IF YOU'RE GOING TO BECOME MY MAN...

AND HERE HE IS!!!

I DON'T THINK THAT'S IT.

...I DO LOOK A BIT DIFFERENT!! MY FRECKLES ARE GONE!!

KLAP KLAP!!

SSSS———— ss

klak

CAPTAIN SMOKER!! TERRIBLE NEWS!!!

MARINE

KLUNK

KRAK!!

KLUNK KLUNK!!

WANTED

PIRATES ARE CAUSING A DISTURBANCE AT THE EXECUTION SCAFFOLD!!!

UH...

THE PIRATES ARE--!!

WH ÜMP!!

splat!!

OH!

DON'T RUN OR YOU'LL DROP THEM.

WOW! THREE SCOOPS!!

TMP TMP TMP

L AKA M

CAP-TAIN...

SHE'S JUST A LITTLE GIRL!!!

PLEASE FOR-GIVE US!!

SHOP

C-CAPTAIN SMOKER!!

M—MY...

...ICE CREAM...

MY PANTS ATE UP ALL YOUR ICE CREAM.

NEXT TIME, TRY FIVE SCOOPS.

KLINK!

SORRY...

WHAP...

SHIVER!!

!!

160

MASTER CHIEF, HERE'S YOUR JACKET.

I'M SORRY!! I'LL GET READY RIGHT AWAY!

TASHIGI!!!! WHERE HAVE YOU BEEN!!?

CAPTAIN SMOKER, SORRY I'M LATE!!

OH...THANK YOU. I'M SO SORRY.

OH, THANK YOU, CHIEF.

TMP TMP TMP TMP

L AKA M

YOU MEAN MORE SO THAN USUAL!!?

I'M A LITTLE OFF TODAY.

FOR-GIVE ME.

YES, SIR!

C'MON. THERE'S A DISTURBANCE AT THE SQUARE!!

MASTER CHIEF PETTY OFFICER TASHIGI
NAVY HEADQUARTERS

161

THERE ARE THREE WANTED INDIVIDUALS IN THE SQUARE.

A CIVILIAN'S BEING HELD HOSTAGE.

WHAT'S GOING ON HERE?

CAPTAIN!! MASTER CHIEF!!

THIRTY MILLION!! BEEN A WHILE SINCE WE HAD ONE LIKE THAT.

WE JUST GOT WORD A FEW DAYS AGO. HE HAS 30 MILLION BERRIES ON HIS HEAD.

LUFFY!? NEVER HEARD OF HIM.

!?

AND MONKEY D. LUFFY.

BUGGY THE CLOWN...

IRON MACE ALVIDA ...

DO

OM!!

...ABOUT TO BE KILLED !!

WELL...

...RIGHT NOW HE'S...

DARN! MY NOSE ITCHES.

LUFFY'S ON THE EXECUTION SCAFFOLD!!!?

DOOM!

WHAT !!?

7.

Luffy's Special Seat

- Captain's chair
- Luffy seems to like this chair. He's always sitting in it.

- He can't swim, so why would he sit in a spot like this? Who knows? But he seems happy, so what's wrong with that?

Nami's Tangerine Grove

- When Nami left Coco Village, she took three of Belle-Mère's tangerine trees with her.
- Nami tends this little orchard.

- But Sanji's the one who protects the trees from tangerine snatchers (like Luffy).
- The tangerines are supposed to be very sweet.

Chapter 99: LUFFY DIED

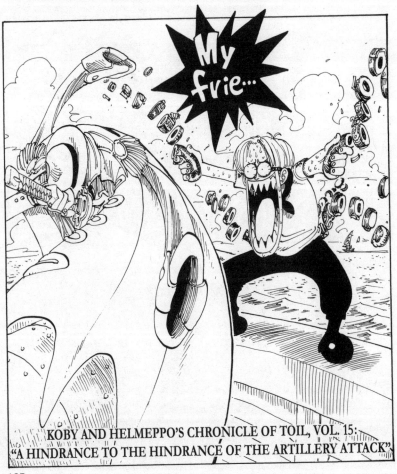

KOBY AND HELMEPPO'S CHRONICLE OF TOIL, VOL. 15:
"A HINDRANCE TO THE HINDRANCE OF THE ARTILLERY ATTACK"

...WERE EVENTS THAT TOOK PLACE IN THE DISTANT PAST.

LEGENDS THAT ENDURE IN THE FUTURE...

WOOOOOO

FOR THAT, HE WILL BE EXECUTED IN GRAND STYLE!!!

DOOM!!

-BWAH HA HA HA HA HA

THE CRIMINAL, M.D. LUFFY, IS GUILTY OF GETTING ON HIS HIGH HORSE AND UPSETTING ME!

HOLD IT RIGHT THERE, YOU PIRATES!!!

HOORAY!!

SO CHEER IN GRAND STYLE!!!

BANG! BANGBANG!!!

WE HAVE BIGGER FISH TO FRY RIGHT NOW.

WE COULD HELP HIM!! AFTER ALL, I DID KILL ONE OF THE BIG FISH OF THE FISH-MEN!!

WHAT GOOD CAN WE DO THERE!?

HEY, WHAT'S THE BIG RUSH!?

BIGGER FISH?

WE SHOULD GO BACK TO THE SQUARE AND HELP LUFFY!

RRMMMBB..

WHAT !!?

A STORM'S GOING TO HIT THIS ISLAND.

HEY!! WAIT UP!!!

OH! THIS REALLY *IS* IMPORTANT!!

IF THERE'S A COMMOTION IN THE SQUARE, THERE'LL BE SOLDIERS.

THIS IS THE CALM BEFORE THE STORM!!

AND I SAW DARK CLOUDS IN THE EASTERN SKY.

THE AIR PRESSURE AND TEMPERATURE HAVE BEEN STEADILY DROPPING.

...WHAT'LL WE DO IF WE TRY TO ESCAPE AND THE BOAT'S GONE!!?

THWUMP!!

CAPTAIN BUGGY HAS PROBABLY EXECUTED HIM IN GRAND STYLE BY NOW.

THIS IS THE RUBBER MAN'S SHIP.

IT'S BIGGER THAN BEFORE.

WHO'S THE ONE THAT RIDES THE RICHIE BIKE?

TELL ME, TELL ME WHO IT IS!!

IT'S ME. ♪

Krshkrsh

RARR!

HOWEVER, IF THE RUBBER MAN ESCAPES, WHICH IS IMPOSSIBLE...

HEH HEH HEH...

SHIK...

BUT IF HE **WERE** TO ESCAPE SOMEHOW, IT'S OUR JOB TO...

RARR

...BURN HIS SHIP. ♪

RARR RARR...

BUT IF WE WAIT...

WHAT'S YOUR HURRY, FOOL?

SHOULD WE ATTACK, SIR?

A DISPUTE BETWEEN PIRATES, EH?

...LET A PIRATE ESCAPE FROM OUR CITY?

RRMMMBB...

HAVE WE EVER...

...SURROUND BUGGY, ALVIDA AND THE REST OF THEM.

NOW LISTEN, WHEN LUFFY'S HEAD ROLLS...

WE'LL LET THOSE PIRATES KILL EACH OTHER.

THEN SHUT UP.

N-NO, NEVER!!

IT'LL MAKE OUR JOB EASY!!

IDIOT! AS IF I'D SPARE YOU!!!

PLEASE DON'T KILL ME!

I'M SORRY!

I'll never do it again

WOoOoo

SO MUCH FOR THE MAN I WAS GOING TO...

HMPH. THIS IS WHAT HAPPENS TO THOSE WHO DEFY US.

AW WELL, NEVER MIND THAT.

...

NO ONE WANTS TO HEAR IT.

YOU HAVE A BIG AUDIENCE.

ANY LAST WORDS?

...

WHAT A DREAMER.

HERE, OF ALL PLACES?

TH oOm

DID HE SAY "KING OF THE PIRATES" !!?

WHAT !!?

STOP THE EXECU-TION !!!!

AAH

AAH

UGH!! U-UGH !!!

WHAM!

WHAM!!

IS THAT ALL YOU HAVE TO SAY, RUBBERHEAD!!?

BUT YOU'RE A SECOND TOO LATE!!

SO YOU'VE COME, ZOLO.

SANJI!!! ZOLO!!!

HELP!!!

IT'S RORONOA ZOLO!

WHAT'S GOING ON!?

...AND HIS PIRATES!!!

ZOLO'S WORKING WITH THAT MONKEY GUY...

WHAT!!?

ER.. BUT...

THE BOUNTY HUNTER? WHAT GREAT TIMING!!

RORONOA ZOLO!? HERE!?

IT'S THAT GUY!!!

GOT IT!!

TEAR DOWN THE SCAFFOLD!!

DON'T TALK NONSENSE. LET'S GET OUTTA HERE.

WE'RE NOT IN THE CLEAR YET.

KLANK

THANK GOOD-NESS.

DO YOU BELIEVE IN A HIGHER POWER?

RUN FOR IT !!!

R A A A H

HERE THEY COME !!

HEY, WHICH WAY!?

SURROUND THE SQUARE AND CAPTURE THE PIRATES!!

DOOM!!

HE SAW HIS DEATH, ACCEPTED IT AND LAUGHED!!

IN THAT MOMENT HE ACCEPTED HIS FATE.

THAT'S NOT IT!!!

WHY DID HE LAUGH? DID HE KNOW HE'D BE RESCUED?

WELL, THAT MONKEY LAUGHED!!!

...EVERY MAN TREMBLES IN FEAR, HOWEVER TOUGH HE IS.

LAUGH!? WHEN FACED WITH CERTAIN DEATH...

SOLDIER, DID YOU EVER SEE A PIRATE LAUGH RIGHT BEFORE HIS EXECUTION?

CAPTAIN!! THE PIRATE ROUND-UP IS...

TWENTY-TWO YEARS AGO, ANOTHER MAN LAUGHED ON THAT VERY SPOT.

HE WAS GOLD ROGER, KING OF THE PIRATES!!!

WOooOooo

THEY WENT BACK TO THE BASE FOR MORE.

THE SUDDEN DOWNPOUR WET THEIR GUNPOWDER.

WAIT, NO...

WHICH WAY DID HE GO?

HE WENT WEST.

THEN THE PORT IS UNPROTECTED!!!

THE FIRST SQUADRON SHOULD BE THERE.

IT'S AS THOUGH SOME KIND OF FORCE IS WILLING THIS MAN'S SURVIVAL !!!

IS THIS JUST A COINCIDENCE ...!!?

THE WIND IS BLOWING TOWARD THE WEST. THEY'LL HAVE A TAILWIND.

I WILL NOT LET HIM LEAVE THIS ISLAND !!!

I, "WHITE CHASE" SMOKER, STAKE MY REPUTATION AS CAPTAIN OF THIS BATTALION.

TO BE CONTINUED IN *ONE PIECE*, VOL. 12!

Pirate Ship

The Merry
Go

Cross-
section
drawing

A four-
cannon
caravel

Anchor
rope

Gun
deck &
storage

x1 Capstan

x1 Men's quarters
(Luffy, Zolo,
Usopp, Sanji)

x1 Women's
quarters
(Nami
and her
treasure)

Bath-
room

x1 Gun deck &
storeroom

x1 Lounge
Galley, conference
room & Bridge

Tiller

Main cannon

Fireproof
Brick wall

Nami's
tangerine
grove

The Merry
Go

Diagram of
work areas

Hammocks
Grog Barrels (water barrels)
Provisions (salted foods, rice,
cheese, etc.)
Treasure
Life preservers

4LDK

No ship's wheel

COMING NEXT VOLUME:

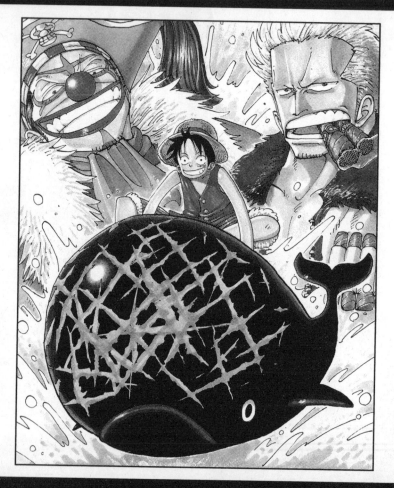

Luffy and his crew are bound for the Grand Line at last, with both newfound enemies and old ones in hot pursuit. Braving a terrible storm, the Straw Hat Pirates make their way toward what they believe is the entrance to the famed sea. But Nami's map is pointing straight up the side of a mountain!

ON SALE NOW!

Story and Art by
KOYOHARU GOTOUGE

In Taisho-era Japan, kindhearted Tanjiro Kamado makes a living selling charcoal. But his peaceful life is shattered when a demon slaughters his entire family. His little sister Nezuko is the only survivor, but she has been transformed into a demon herself! Tanjiro sets out on a dangerous journey to find a way to return his sister to normal and destroy the demon who ruined his life.

THE ACTION-PACKED SUPERHERO COMEDY ABOUT ONE MAN'S AMBITION TO BE A HERO FOR FUN!

ONE-PUNCH MAN

STORY BY
ONE

ART BY
YUSUKE MURATA

Nothing about Saitama passes the eyeball test when it comes to superheroes, from his lifeless expression to his bald head to his unimpressive physique. However, this average-looking guy has a not-so-average problem—he just can't seem to find an opponent strong enough to take on!

Can he finally find an opponent who can go toe-to-toe with him and give his life some meaning? Or is he doomed to a life of superpowered boredom?

www.viz.com

SHOYO HINATA IS OUT TO PROVE THAT IN VOLLEYBALL YOU DON'T NEED TO BE TALL TO FLY!

HAIKYU!!

Story and Art by HARUICHI FURUDATE

Ever since he saw the legendary player known as the "Little Giant" compete at the national volleyball finals, Shoyo Hinata has been aiming to be the best volleyball player ever! He decides to join the team at the high school the Little Giant went to—and then surpass him. Who says you need to be tall to play volleyball when you can jump higher than anyone else?

You're Reading in the Wrong Direction!!

Whoops! Guess what? You're starting at the wrong end of the comic!

...It's true! In keeping with the original Japanese format, **One Piece** is meant to be read from right to left, starting in the upper-right corner.

Unlike English, which is read from left to right, Japanese is read from right to left, meaning that action, sound effects and word-balloon order are completely reversed... something which can make readers unfamiliar with Japanese feel pretty backwards themselves. For this reason, manga or Japanese comics published in the U.S. in English have sometimes been published "flopped"—that is, printed in exact reverse order, as though seen from the other side of a mirror.

By flopping pages, U.S. publishers can avoid confusing readers, but the compromise is not without its downside. For one thing, a character in a flopped manga series who once wore in the original Japanese version a T-shirt emblazoned with "M A Y" (as in "the merry month of") now wears one which reads "Y A M"! Additionally, many manga creators in Japan are themselves unhappy with the process, as some feel the mirror-imaging of their art skews their original intentions.

We are proud to bring you Eiichiro Oda's **One Piece** in the original unflopped format. For now, though, turn to the other side of the book and let the journey begin...!

—Editor